Lyonel Feininger   The Ruin by the Sea

Introduction by Eila Kokkinen

Selections of Drawings and Prints   Edited by William S. Lieberman

The Museum of Modern Art, New York

Introduction

From 1924 through 1935, Lyonel Feininger spent summer vacations at Deep in Pomerania on the Baltic coast, now in East Germany. Sometimes accompanied by members of his family but often alone, he reserved these months for drawings and watercolors as a respite from easel painting. A wild and unpopulated resort, Deep lacked the comforts of previous vacation spots. Nonetheless, Feininger was annually drawn back by its deserted beaches and the variable and stormy climate which produced a spectacle of changing sea and sky. Walking along the wind-swept beach and sketching the sea in its many aspects were a part of his daily life at Deep.*

While there, on July 11, 1928, during an excursion to the nearby village of Hoff in the company of his second son Laurence, Feininger spotted a curious structure at the top of a cliff overlooking the sea, and described it in a letter to his wife, Julia:

---

*One of Feininger's sons, T. Lux Feininger, has discussed the period at Deep in "Lyonel Feininger in West-Deep," *Baltische Studien*, Neue Folge, Band 49, 1962/1963, pp. 101-120.

"The coast is high and steep, beautifully vast in lines, but large stretches are crumbling away, for the rains have caused landslides. Far away, at the highest and steepest point stood something puzzling, a bulky cube which might have been a fort but, in fact, was quite something else. There on top of the edge of the precipice, and without a doubt doomed to perdition, stood the ruins of a church. I was completely mystified. Using my Zeiss field glasses I studied the thing, I made sketches, and visions of pictures arose in my mind. Successively as we approached, apertures revealed buttresses, and at last a row of beautifully shaped arched window-openings in the Gothic style came into view. It all seemed so magnificent, and full of magic. Coming closer, and when finally quite near I saw that in sober reality the walls were barely twenty-four feet high, but I could not be disenchanted, for me they seemed monumental as in a big cathedral."

The ruin that intrigued Feininger has been documented in the state archives for the county of Stettin, Pomerania. Records indicate a church existed there as early as 1331, and beyond it, three farms extended north to the sea. When its vault, originally built on Gothic arches, collapsed in later years, the building was bricked over and a wooden roof added. It acquired a nondescript appearance and retained only the Gothic windows of the choir. Gradually but inexorably, the sea approached, eroding and inundating the farms. By 1868, the sea had eaten

The church at Hoff before 1900

its way at the bottom of the cliff to within a few feet of the church. At that time, a visitor recounts, the path leading to the church on the sea side was still visible but unsafe to approach. He mentions attending a service at the church and found that although the windows facing the sea were boarded up, the sermon was made inaudible by the roar of the surf. Dams and palings failed to save the building from destruction, and it was abandoned in 1874. Falls carrying off the northwest corner, the north wall, and half of the west gable occurred in 1900, 1901, and 1903. When Feininger saw it, only the south wall and a portion of the choir remained standing.

On the day of his discovery, Feininger recorded the visit with twelve small pencil sketches of the ruin (pages 10-13, 18, 22, 23, 25), which became studies for works to follow. In August 1928, he did several pen and ink drawings concentrating on two main views of the ruin (pages 14, 15, 19). Defining form in exact, ruled lines as in some of his seascapes and drawings of ships, he created a strong structural tension and, mysteriously, a sense of atmosphere and light. In August 1929, again at Deep, he completed two richly textured charcoal drawings, fusing sky, church, and cliff in planes of light and shadow (pages 16, 20); these form composition studies for two major paintings.

In a letter to his wife dated June 4, 1932, Feininger pinpointed the relationship of drawing to his painting:

"In the medium of charcoal I have discovered a great relationship with pure painting. Jotting down one's first nebulous, chaotic conceptions, one gradually can work...through to firm ground and precise form. That which has been halfway indicated is open to further evolution. Nothing is quite definite until it has reached final clarity in the finished painting in oil."

Feininger preferred to complete his oil paintings in surroundings removed from his subject, believing that its proximity bound him too closely to literal appearance. Away from Deep, in

January 1930, he finished his first painting of the ruin (page 21). Long thought to be lost, this painting recently came to light and was acquired by The Museum of Modern Art. It combines several views of the ruin, and the planes suggested in the charcoal drawings are given clarity and distinctness but retain a sense of soft, diffused light. The arches repeated against the sky, like reflections in water, are restored to their Gothic splendor.

The artist revisited the ruin in 1932, this time with his son, Andreas (whose photographs of the ruin are reproduced below), and in 1934. A new group of sketches (pages 9, 24, 26) done

Photographs of the ruin by Andreas Feininger. Left, view from the north; right, view from the east

on the spot is followed by two watercolors of 1934 (page 17) and several charcoal drawings of 1935 (pages 27, 30). The broad view of the ruin facing the steep cliff is now emphasized.

In 1937, after living nearly fifty years in Germany, Feininger returned to his homeland, the United States. In 1940 he painted an impressive second version of the ruin, and in 1953 he executed from memory several larger watercolors, achieving a delicate dematerialization of form (pages 28, 29). The ruin still preoccupied the artist during his last years, and left unfinished at his death was a small tentative painting in oil (page 31) after the composition of the painting of 1940. With the exception of a major group of paintings and drawings of the church at Gelmeroda in Thuringia, no other architectural subject had interested Feininger so continuously and resulted in such a large group of works.

The series numbers some thirty drawings and watercolors and three paintings, of which twenty-three are illustrated here. They reveal the fascinating metamorphosis of the ruin from factual reality to the precise and pure delineation of form characteristic of Feininger's work.

EILA KOKKINEN

July 17, 1934

July 11, 1928

July 11, 1928

11

with Lawrence
1 7 28

again, with Andrew
on Thurs. Jy. 28. 1932

July 11, 1928

13

Feininger

Ruine am Meere I

14

August 6, 1928

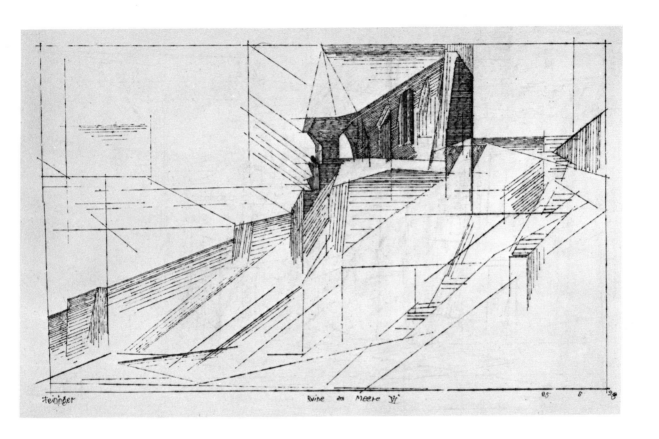

Feininger   Ruine am Meere VI

August 25, 1928

15

Feininger   Composition for painting: "Ruin on the Cliff"   20. August, 1929

16

August 20, 1929

1934

18

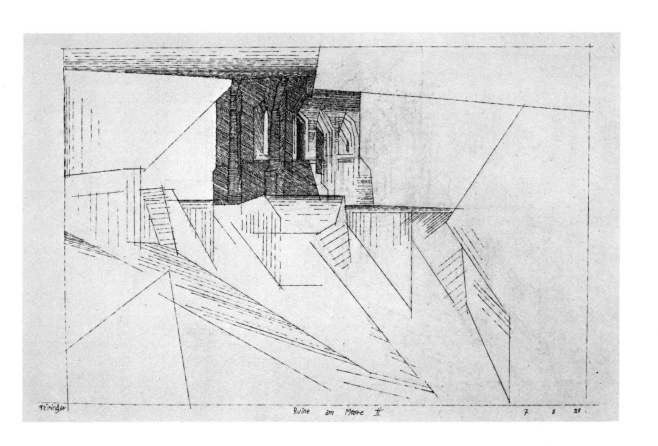

Ruine am Meere II

Feininger

7 8 28

August 7, 1928

19

Feininger

Ruine an Meere I

21 . 8 . 29

20

1930

22

July 11, 1928

24

July 11, 1928

25

Feininger

26

Feininger   The Ruin on the Cliff   1935

1935

church on the cliff

church on the cliffs.

1953

30

n.d.

List of Illustrations

Unless otherwise indicated, the works listed are the gift of Mrs. Lyonel Feininger to The Museum of Modern Art. Titles in italics are those inscribed on the works by the artist; dates in parentheses are not inscribed. In dimensions, height precedes width; sheet size is given for works on paper.

Photograph Credits

All photographs are by Soichi Sunami, with the following exceptions. Andreas Feininger: 7; James Mathews: 5, 31; Rolf Petersen: 15, 23; Malcolm Varon: cover and 17, 9, 21, 29.